UNSPOKEN STRUGGLES

My Journey to Find My Voice

ERIC B. BROWN

www.TrueVinePublishing.org

Unspoken Struggles
Eric B. Brown

Published by
True Vine Publishing Company
810 Dominican Dr.
Nashville TN 37228
www.TrueVinePublishing.org

ISBN: 978-1-968092-51-1 Paperback
ISBN: 978-1-968092-52-8 eBook

Printed in the United States of America.
For information, contact the author.

DEDICATION

This book is dedicated to my wife, Shari P. Brown, my partner of thirty-two years and the steady rock God placed in my life. Through every season, moments of joy and seasons of struggle, she has remained faithful, steadfast, and full of grace. "Two are better than one...for if either of them falls, the one will lift up his companion" (Ecclesiastes 4:9–10).

She has walked with me through the unseen battles, believed in me when my voice felt silenced, and stood firm when the weight of the journey was heavy. Her strength has been a reflection of God's sustaining hand, reminding me that "a cord of three strands is not quickly broken" (Ecclesiastes 4:12).

Her love and encouragement gave me the courage to tell this story. She inspired me to write when fear tried to keep me quiet, and she reminded me that "He who began a good work in you will carry it on to completion" (Philippians 1:6).

For all you are, all we have endured together, and all God has yet to unfold, this book is for you.

I love you to life, Shari B. "Many women do noble things, but you surpass them all" (Proverbs 31:29).

ACKNOWLEDGEMENT

Although my name appears as the author, this work is the fruit of divine grace. Apart from God the Father, through God the Son, and by the power of the Holy Spirit, none of this would exist. I offer all glory to God Almighty, who called, sustained, and authored this work through me. What is written here is not born of human wisdom or effort, but of obedience to His leading and faithfulness to His purpose. My prayer is that the Lord would use these pages to reach those whose voices have been silenced, that they may be heard, restored, and drawn closer to the truth of Christ.

TABLE OF CONTENTS

INTRODUCTION

For most of my life, I carried a truth I was afraid to say out loud: I could not read.

I learned early how to disappear in plain sight. In classrooms filled with confident voices reading aloud, I mastered silence. I memorized patterns, avoided eye contact, and found ways to stay unnoticed. What looked like compliance was survival. What felt like failure became shame I learned to hide.

Sports became my refuge. On the field, I did not need words. Athletics leveled the playing field and gave me something I could excel at when reading failed me. Sports were not just games; they were a lifeline. They gave me identity, acceptance, and a place where I could belong without being exposed.

To protect my secret, I created conflict. Acting out became a distraction, a way to redirect attention away from what I could not do. Home carried its own weight, and many days ended in exhaustion rather than understanding. Still, even then, I prayed. Sometimes with words. Sometimes with tears. Gratitude became a quiet habit long before it ever became a lifestyle.

One of the most painful moments of my childhood came when I had to repeat seventh grade. Shame settled deep, and I believed that repeating a grade meant repeating failure. I tried to outrun that feeling by leaving, hoping distance could erase what I carried inside. It did not. Truth has a way of finding you, and it was in that season that I began to understand the connection between truth and freedom.

God met me in places where I felt invisible. Slowly, and often quietly, He began healing my self-image. What I believed about myself started to change. Not all at once, but enough to keep me moving forward.

Along the way, people entered my life who did not know they were rescuing me, but they were. Through observation, trust, and relationship, hope began to take root. I started to see that my struggle did not disqualify me. It was shaping me.

This book is not just about learning to read. It is about learning to live. It is about discovering that progress is possible, even in the places you never talk about. It is about finding your voice after years of silence.

After I volunteered at several elementary schools across Florida, Georgia, and South Carolina, I couldn't help but notice how many students struggled with reading. Their frustration and hesitancy brought back memories of myself at their age, the confusion, the fear of being called on, the silent wish that someone would help.

What I later learned through national data gave words to what my heart already knew was a crisis. Today, approximately 21% of American adults, roughly 43 million people, are classified as having very limited literacy skills, struggling with basic reading tasks. Even more staggering, about 54% of adults read below a sixth-grade level, making everyday reading, like instructions, forms, even simple stories, a significant challenge for many.

These numbers are not just statistics; they represent millions of stories of silence, missed opportunities, and unspoken pain. And that pain is familiar to me, because I once lived in it.

As I reflect on my own journey and look out at this great nation, I feel compelled by something much greater than ambition. I feel called by God to go, not just across the South, but around the country, to bring this book and this message to those who cannot read it for themselves. It is my mission to help those who are trapped in illiteracy to find their voice, their confidence, and ultimately, their freedom.

Jesus told His disciples to go into all the world, to bring hope where there was despair. Just as they stepped into the unknown with faith as their compass, I, too, step forward, not in my own strength, but in the power of God, to reach those who need someone to read the words of life with them, for them, and through them.

Jesus also told Peter, "Now that you have been restored, go back and strengthen your brothers." Those words are not just Scripture to me, they are instruction.

Now that I have been brought under this covenant, now that God has blessed me with the ability to read and to write, I understand my assignment. I am called to go back. I am called to strengthen those who are still standing where I once stood, those who struggle to read, to write, and to find their voice.

What God has done for me was never meant to stop with me. It was preparation. It was purpose. And it was proof. I believe with all my heart that the same God who met me in my unspoken struggles will meet you in yours. What once held you silent will not define you forever. What you could not say, what you could not read, what you could not understand, God is able to restore.

Your unspoken struggles will not have the final word. They will become your testimony.

If you are carrying a hidden struggle, wrestling with shame, or searching for purpose, this story is written for you. My prayer is that as you turn these pages, you will find the courage to face your own unspoken battles and, in time, discover your voice, too.

Three Core Truths of the Book

1. It's Not Where You Start or How You Start, It's How You Finish

Your origin does not define your outcome. *Unspoken Struggles* challenges the lie that early disadvantages determine lifelong limits. This book emphasizes resilience, growth, and the power of endurance, showing that the finish line is shaped by persistence, not your point of entry.

2. Surround Yourself with Good People

No one finds their voice alone. This journey highlights the importance of relationships, mentors, friends, teachers, and encouragers, who speak life when you don't yet know how.

The right people can help you see yourself clearly before you ever see it for yourself.

3. It Takes a Village to Raise a Child

This book honors the truth that healing and development are communal efforts.

Whether by family, faith leaders, educators, or unexpected helpers, it is often a village that fills the gaps left behind. *Unspoken Struggles* reminds us that community can rewrite a child's story, and an adult's future.

"Being confident of this very thing, that He who has "... begun a good work in you will complete it" (Philippians 1:6).

CHAPTER 1

Elementary Days — Learning to Disappear

"Eric."

The sound of my name landed heavier than it should have. The classroom was quiet enough that I could hear the scrape of chair legs against the floor and the faint hum of the lights overhead. My eyes stayed locked on the book in front of me, though I hadn't read a single word on the page.

"Eric," the teacher said again, gentler this time. "Come up here and read the next paragraph."

My chest tightened. Time slowed. The room felt smaller, closing in around my desk. I could feel the heat rising in my face, my palms already damp. I knew what waited for me at the front of that room: rows of faces, letters that made no sense, and the moment when everyone would realize what I already knew.

I couldn't read.

As I stood, my mind raced through options. Maybe I could pretend to be sick. Maybe I could ask to use the bathroom. Maybe I could stall long enough for her to change her mind. Each step toward the front felt longer than the last, my heart pounding so loudly I was sure the whole class could hear it.

I glanced sideways and saw the chalkboard. I imagined the book in my hands, the letters blurring together, refusing to line up in any order I could understand. I imagined the whispers. The laughter that would try to hide itself. The looks.

No. I couldn't let that happen.

So I did the only thing I knew how to do. I turned and swung.

The fight was quick and loud. A sudden burst of motion in a room that moments earlier had been still. Desks shifted. Voices rose. The teacher rushed forward, breaking us apart, her voice sharp now, filled with disappointment. I didn't hear most of what she said. All I knew was that I wasn't reading anymore.

Violence became my escape route. A fight felt safer than standing still in front of my shame.

Back then, I didn't have language for what I was feeling. I didn't know it was fear or embarrassment or desperation. I just knew I couldn't let anyone see how far behind I was. What adults saw as bad behavior was really a silent plea: please don't make me read.

Elementary school was not crayons and coloring books for me. It was a daily exercise in survival. Each morning, I walked into Bethune Elementary School in Hollywood,

Florida, carrying a weight far heavier than my small frame should have known. The smell of chalk hung thick in the air. Wooden desks sat in neat rows, and children flipped pages with ease, their fingers tracing words they understood.

Their voices floated confidently when it was their turn to read aloud. Hands shot up eagerly. When the teacher called on them, pride filled the room. When she called on me, my stomach twisted into knots so tight I could barely breathe.

I would stare at the page, the letters scattered like puzzle pieces that refused to fit. My classmates didn't understand. How could they? Children are honest, sometimes painfully so.

"Why is he so slow?"

"He can't even read that?"

"Something must be wrong with him."

Every word carved something into me. Not smart. Not capable. Not enough.

The truth was, I wasn't lazy. I wasn't uninterested. I wasn't behind because I wanted to be. I needed help nobody knew how to give, and I didn't yet have a voice to ask for it.

I learned how to hide. I memorized the first sentence the teacher read and repeated it when it was my turn, praying she wouldn't notice my voice shaking. Sometimes it worked. Many times it didn't.

I can still see her eyes—kind, concerned—as she said, "Try again, sweetheart. Start at the top."

But I didn't know where the top was.

Recess became my refuge. The playground didn't judge me. The swings didn't care what I could or couldn't read. The basketball court didn't laugh when I stumbled over words. Out there, for a few precious minutes, I could just be a kid.

Still, the shadow followed me. I knew the bell would ring. I knew the books would open again. I knew tomorrow would bring another moment where I'd be called to prove something I couldn't yet do.

Even then, beneath the fear and frustration, something quiet was forming inside me. A stubborn kind of determination. A will to survive. I didn't understand it at the time, but my life was already telling a story shaped by struggle but not defeated by it.

I couldn't read the words on the page, but I was learning how to read people. I was learning how to endure pressure. I was learning how to stand, even when standing meant being misunderstood.

I didn't know God the way I would later. I didn't have the language for faith or calling. But I prayed anyway. Sometimes with words. Sometimes with tears. Gratitude began quietly, long before it became a lifestyle.

Those elementary years, the ones that hurt the most, were teaching me something I wouldn't recognize until much later. Silence was not the end of my story. It was the beginning of a voice still forming, one shaped in classrooms where I felt invisible, and strengthened in moments when I refused to quit—even when quitting felt easier.

This chapter of my life began with fear and avoidance, with fists instead of words, and with a boy doing everything he could to hide what he couldn't yet fix.

CHAPTER 2

Finding Refuge — When Sports Gave Me a Place to Belong

"Eric, get in there."

Coach's voice cut through the noise of the field, sharp and certain. I hesitated for half a second, not because I was scared, but because I wasn't used to being called forward for something good. In the classroom, being called meant exposure. Out here, it meant opportunity.

The helmet felt oversized on my head, the chin strap tight against my jaw. My heart thumped hard, but it wasn't dread this time. It was something else. Anticipation. I jogged onto the field, grass crunching under my cleats, the late afternoon sun pressing down on my back. The air smelled like sweat and dirt, and for once, that smell didn't make me want to disappear.

No one handed me a book. No one waited for me to speak.

All I had to do was line up.

The ball snapped, bodies collided, and instinct took over. I ran, hit, blocked, and pushed forward with everything I had. When the whistle blew, I was breathing hard, chest burning, legs aching, and smiling. Nobody laughed. Nobody whispered. Nobody asked me to prove myself with words I didn't have.

On the field, I belonged.

Football didn't ask me to explain myself. It didn't care what I struggled with inside a classroom. It only asked one question: Were you willing to give effort? I could answer that without hesitation.

Before football, school felt like something I had to survive. After football, it became something I had a reason to stay connected to. I still struggled to read. That didn't change overnight. The letters still blurred. The fear still crept in when books opened. But now, quitting had consequences I cared about. If I wanted to stay on the team, I had to show up everywhere else, too.

The coaches noticed things in me I didn't see in myself. They didn't measure me by reading levels or test scores. They measured heart. Discipline. Willingness to keep getting back up after getting knocked down. Every practice was a lesson in focus. Every drill reinforced structure. Every correction came with expectation instead of condemnation.

For the first time, adults weren't just pointing out what I couldn't do. They were calling out what I could.

Out there, I wasn't "the boy who couldn't read." I was a teammate. A player. Someone who mattered to the group. That feeling did something inside me. It didn't erase the shame, but it challenged it. It gave me a new identity to hold onto when the old one tried to pull me under.

Because I wanted to stay on the field, I tried harder in the classroom. Not because reading suddenly made sense, but because purpose has a way of pushing you forward even when understanding lags behind. Football gave my days structure. It gave my mind something to organize around. It gave me a reason not to disappear.

Looking back now, I can see what I couldn't see then. God used a game to keep me connected to school. He planted confidence in a place where insecurity had been growing. He gave me a space where I could learn discipline before I ever learned doctrine.

But the field wasn't the only place shaping me.

By the time practices ended and the sun dipped lower, the streets called. Collins Apartments, what we proudly called "the Greens," became our second field of play. The pavement was cracked, the rims bent just enough to make every shot a challenge, and pride was always on the line. We ran streetball hard, playing for reputation as much as points.

When we could, we took that same energy to the teen center, then known as Northeast Community Center, now the Dr. Martin Luther King Jr. Community Center. That place wasn't just about sports. It was about survival. About brotherhood. About learning the rules of a world that didn't always feel forgiving.

You had to be tough. You had to stand your ground. You couldn't show weakness. We loved each other in our own way, through competition, through trash talk, through loyalty that didn't need explaining. Long before I understood who I was in God, I was learning who I was among my brothers on those concrete courts.

Back then, being "hard-core" meant never letting anyone see fear in your eyes. The streets taught me how to be strong on the outside. Later, God would teach me how to be strong on the inside.

I didn't know it at the time, but the same boy learning how to take hits on the field and the court was being prepared for something heavier. Something deeper. Sports gave me refuge, but they weren't the destination. They were training ground.

I was learning discipline without calling it that. Learning endurance without naming it. Learning teamwork before I ever learned how to ask for help.

The game gave me confidence. The streets gave me toughness. But neither would be enough on their own.

There was still something broken beneath the pads and bravado. Still a fear I hadn't named. Still a struggle waiting for me the next time a teacher called my name and expected me to read.

And that struggle wasn't finished with me yet.

CHAPTER 3

After the Bell — Love That Didn't Need Words

The house was quiet when I pushed the door open. Not the peaceful kind of quiet. The waiting kind.

My backpack slid off my shoulder and hit the floor with a soft thud. The sun coming through the window stretched across the living room, landing on furniture worn smooth by years of use. I stood there for a moment, listening. No voices. No television. Just the low hum of the refrigerator and the distant sound of traffic outside.

Mama was still at work.

Daddy, too.

I went straight to the kitchen. The cabinets looked the same as they always did, familiar, honest. I opened the refrigerator already knowing what I would find, but still hoping, just a little, that today might be different.

It wasn't.

I pulled out two slices of bread and squeezed mayonnaise across the middle, spreading it thin so it would last. I called it a wish sandwich. I wished there was meat. I wished dinner was closer. I wished, sometimes, that I could ask for more without feeling like I was asking for too much.

I sat at the small table and ate slowly, listening for the front door, knowing it wouldn't open for a while. Homework stayed tucked in my bag. Not because I didn't care, but because there was no one at home who could help me with it. That wasn't anybody's fault. It was just the way things were.

My parents worked hard, harder than I understood at the time. My mother, Vera Humphrey, left early in the mornings to clean houses in Hollywood and Hallandale Beach. She scrubbed floors and wiped down kitchens that weren't hers so we could have food on our table. My father, James Humphrey, took whatever work he could find. For a long time, that meant unloading boxcars for lumber companies, labor that bent your back and numbed your hands. Later, he found steadier work as a maintenance technician with the City of Dania Beach.

Neither of them had the opportunity to go far in school. My father had only a third-grade education. My mother finished high school. There was no one at home who could sit beside me and walk me through assignments or explain the words that confused me. That absence was never neglect. It was reality.

Still, we never went without what mattered most.

There was always food to eat, even if it was simple. There were always clothes on our backs, even if they came from Zayre's or Kmart department stores. The lights stayed on. The house stayed clean. And every day, my parents showed up, even when they were tired, even when life asked more of them than it gave back.

They didn't complain. They didn't explain how heavy things felt. They didn't narrate their sacrifice. They just did what needed to be done.

My mother was born and raised in Charleston, South Carolina, in Mt. Pleasant, what she called "four mile." My father came from Blakely, Georgia. Both were raised in a time when Black folks worked the fields, labored with their hands, and survived more than they dreamed. College wasn't part of their story. Opportunity was limited. But love wasn't.

Their love didn't sound like encouragement speeches or long talks at the table. It sounded like early mornings. It felt like tired hands. It looked like consistency.

When Mama came home later in the evening, her body carried the weight of the day, but she still asked if we had eaten. When Daddy walked through the door, shoulders heavy, he still checked on us, still made sure we were okay. They didn't ask many questions. They didn't pry. They loved us in the way they knew how, by providing.

Looking back now, I realize how much of my childhood was shaped by struggles that were never spoken out loud. My parents didn't talk about what they didn't have. They didn't frame life in terms of lack. They simply kept going.

That quiet steadiness held me together during years when I felt confused, ashamed, and unseen. Even when I couldn't explain what I was struggling with, even when I didn't have the words to ask for help, their presence gave me something solid to stand on.

I didn't understand it then, but the foundation they laid mattered. The discipline I learned at home showed up later in places I didn't expect. The endurance I watched them live out would one day be required of me. The love they modeled, steady, sacrificial, unannounced, became a blueprint I would carry forward.

Life after the bell wasn't easy. It wasn't polished. But it was real. And it was enough.

That house, those meals, those long workdays, they were teaching me something no classroom ever did. They taught me that love doesn't always speak. Sometimes it shows up quietly, day after day, and holds you together when you don't yet know how to hold yourself.

CHAPTER 4

The Year I Had to Repeat Seventh Grade

Middle school was supposed to be a fresh start. That was the story I told myself as I walked through those halls for the first time. New building. New teachers. New faces. I believed that if everything around me changed, maybe what I carried inside wouldn't follow me.

It did.

The hallways were wider than anything I remembered from elementary school. Lockers lined the walls like steel sentries. The noise was louder. The crowds moved faster. Everyone seemed to know where they were going, and I moved with them, careful not to stand out too much. Middle school had rules I didn't yet understand, and I felt the pressure immediately. The expectations were higher. The margin for hiding was smaller.

Sixth grade reminded me quickly of what I already knew, but hoped I could forget. I was behind.

Reading assignments came faster. Comprehension was assumed. Teachers spoke as if we were all starting from the same place. I smiled in the hallways. I joked when I needed to. I blended in as best I could. Inside, the fear stayed close. I could run on a football field without hesitation, but a paragraph on a page still stopped me cold.

Middle school tested more than my education. It tested my identity.

I became aware of my skin in a way I hadn't been before. Being a dark-skinned boy already felt like walking through the world with a target on my back. Add my academic struggle to that, and I felt exposed from every angle. The jokes came quietly at first, whispered just loud enough for me to hear. Then they came boldly, thrown like stones in crowded hallways.

Smokey the Bear.

Blackie.

Spook.

Each name carried weight. Each one landed where it was meant to. Middle school had a way of finding your differences and using them against you. Kids could sense weakness. They circled it. I learned how to laugh when I wanted to cry. I learned how to stand straight even when everything in me wanted to shrink.

One day, something shifted.

The joke came like it always did, careless and sharp. My heart started racing. My hands shook. My feet stayed planted. I looked at the one who said it and spoke before fear could stop me.

"That's not my name."

My voice was not loud. It was steady. The hallway went quiet for just a moment. Fear surged through me, but strength rose with it. That moment did not end the teasing. It did change something inside me. I realized I did not have to accept every label thrown my way.

The battles continued. My struggle with reading grew heavier as the work became harder. By the time I reached seventh grade, the gap felt impossible to close. My classmates moved forward. They read aloud. They wrote paragraphs. They followed lessons with ease. I watched and tried to keep up.

Every day felt like climbing uphill with no air in my lungs.

Tests made my chest tighten. I stared at papers, not because I didn't care, but because I did not know where to begin. Homework followed me home like a shadow. Grades posted on walls felt like announcements of my fear made public.

I told myself to keep pushing. I told myself it would click eventually. I told myself not to quit.

Then came the day that changed everything.

"Eric," the counselor said gently, "you're going to have to repeat the seventh grade."

The words settled slowly, then hit all at once. Repeating a grade felt like repeating my pain. Shame rushed in before I could stop it. My face burned. Tears pressed hard behind my eyes. Questions flooded my mind faster than answers ever had.

What was wrong with me?

Who was going to laugh?

Would I ever move forward?

Repeating seventh grade felt like confirmation of every fear I had tried to outrun. It told me that no matter how hard I worked, no matter how much effort I gave, I still wasn't enough.

That year marked me.

It marked how I saw myself. It marked how I measured my worth. It marked the beginning of a belief I would carry for far too long, that I was always behind, always catching up, always one step away from being exposed.

At the time, I did not see it as a lesson. I saw it as failure.

I did not know then that this year would become a turning point. All I knew was the weight of it. The embarrassment. The fear. The quiet resolve to survive another year in a place that already felt unforgiving.

Seventh grade did not break me.

It did leave a scar.

And that scar would shape every step I took next.

Failure is not final, it is formation. The seventh grade did not end my story; it interpreted it long enough to mark me. That year left a scar, not as proof of the feat, but as evidence that I survive what could have silenced me.

Scars don't disappear, they teach the body how to heal stronger. What felt like falling behind was actually a forced paused, shaping my resolve, sharpening my awareness, and redirecting my steps. I did not repeat a grade, I repeated a lesson, and this time I learned that failure is not a verdict, it is a teacher. It doesn't define where you end, it defines how you rise.

CHAPTER 5

Running South — When Distance Felt Like Freedom

I asked my mother if I could go to Charleston the same way a man asks for air when he feels like he is drowning.

It didn't come out dramatic. I didn't explain everything I was feeling. I just said I wanted to visit my grandmother for a while. I needed a change. I needed space. I needed to get away from Florida.

Mama looked at me for a long moment. She didn't ask many questions. She nodded and said yes.

I took that yes and built a whole new future around it.

Charleston felt different the moment I arrived. The air moved slower. The streets felt quieter. Nobody knew my school record. Nobody knew I was repeating seventh grade. Nobody looked at me like I was behind. For the first time in a long time, I felt like I could breathe.

I told people I was moving on to the eighth grade. The words came easily. Too easily. I said them enough times that they started to feel true. In Charleston, I could be whoever I said I was. I could leave the embarrassment behind and step into a version of myself that did not carry the weight of being held back.

Days passed without reminders of failure. There were no teachers calling my name. No tests placed in front of me. No grades posted for everyone to see. Just family, familiar streets, and the comfort of being somewhere that did not demand answers from me.

For a while, the shame stayed quiet. But summer has a way of ending whether you are ready or not. One afternoon, my mother showed up. I saw her before I heard her voice. The sight of her standing there told me everything before she said a word. My chest tightened. The lie I had been living started to collapse in on itself.

It was time to go back.

The drive back to Florida felt longer than the trip north. The closer we got, the heavier everything became. The truth I had tried to outrun was waiting right where I left it. Charleston was never an escape. It was a pause. Florida was still there. School was still there. Seventh grade was still there.

I went back knowing I could not pretend anymore. The version of myself I created in Charleston could not survive the return. I had to face what I had been avoiding. I had to sit in classrooms where the work was harder than before. I had to walk hallways where people would notice that I was still there when others had moved on.

Changing locations did not change my reality. That summer taught me something I did not yet have words for:

distance can hide pain, but it cannot heal it. Pretending can quiet shame for a season, but it always demands repayment.

When I stepped back into Florida, I carried more than embarrassment. I carried the understanding that running had limits. I could not outrun the truth of where I was. I could only decide how I would face it.

I did not feel stronger yet. I did not feel wiser. I felt exposed. I had learned that hiding cost energy I did not have. I had learned that pretending to be ahead only made the fall harder. I had learned that freedom was not found in distance.

It was found in facing what I wanted to avoid. I did not know it then, but that realization would change the way I moved forward. The lie had run its course. The truth was back in front of me. And this time, I could not look away. Later in life came Kent Richard Hanna, one of the most impactful voices I've ever encountered. I eventually coached side-by-side with him, and I still quote some of his mottos:

"Every play is a new day."

"As long as I've got life, health, and strength, I'll be all right."

His teachings didn't just stay on the field; they anchored themselves in my mind and spirit.

CHAPTER 6

Borrowed Voices — The Friends Who Helped Me Survive

I remember the sound of their voices before I remember their faces.

We were sitting in the teen center, the kind of place where conversations bounced off concrete walls and laughter carried farther than it should have. Someone asked a question. I don't remember what it was. What I remember is how quickly the answer came.

James spoke first. I watched James answer questions with authority that made people lean in. He didn't rush his words, and he didn't second-guess himself. When James spoke, it sounded like he believe what he was saying before anyone else had a chance to.

Antonio was different but just as powerful. He was calmer, measured, breaking the idea down in a way that made it easy to understand. He didn't rush. He paused before he spoke, as if weighing every word, choosing language with care and intention. He didn't show off. He spoke like someone who knew where he was going.

I didn't say anything. I listened closely to the rhythm of their speech, the phrases they used, the confidence and their tone, and even the way they carried themselves. That became my habit. Wherever James and Antonio were, I positioned myself close enough to hear. Not because I wanted to copy them, but because I needed to learn how they moved through the world. They weren't just smart. They were comfortable being smart. They walked into rooms without shrinking. They spoke without ssecond-guessing themselves.

Where I struggled, they excelled. Instead of making me feel smaller, they made the space feel safer. They laughed at me sometimes. James laughed hard. I remember one day when I went into the teen center to show my grades to Miss Rose. My chest felt tight. Tears came before I could stop them. I looked up and saw James laughing like the moment was pure comedy.

But the laughter didn't last. Neither James nor Antonio judged me. They didn't push me away. They didn't let me quit. They stayed. That mattered more than the laughter ever could.

They couldn't fix what I was dealing with. They couldn't magically make reading easier or school feel fair. What they gave me was something different. Proximity. Example. Confidence I could borrow.

I memorized sound before I understood structure. I learned people before I learned pages. When it was my turn to speak, I used what I had stored up. I repeated phrases I had heard them use. I mimicked their tone. I leaned on their confidence when mine felt thin. To the outside world, it probably looked like I knew what I was talking about. Inside, I was surviving.

People say fake it until you make it. At the time, that's exactly what it felt like. I was faking understanding. Faking confidence. Faking intelligence. But what people couldn't see was the work happening underneath. I was paying attention. I was learning. I was building something slowly.

What looked like pretending was preparation. James and Antonio didn't sit me down and teach me lessons. They taught by being themselves. They showed me how intelligence sounded. How confidence carried itself. How to speak without apology.

Little by little, something changed. I started believing the words when I said them. I started trusting my voice even when it wasn't fully formed. I stopped shrinking in conversations. I stopped assuming I didn't belong.

I still struggled. That didn't disappear. Reading was still hard. School was still exhausting. But now I had language and rhythm. I had examples to follow.

Listening became my classroom. Those friendships did more than help me sound smarter. They helped me see myself differently. I wasn't broken. I was learning in a different order.

I did not find my voice all at once. It came piece by piece through observation, repetition, and trust. James and Antonio never knew the role they played. They never knew how closely I watched or how carefully I listened. To them, we were just friends spending time together. To me, they were lifelines.

35

They held me up until I could stand on my own, and even then, the voice I was building was still forming, but for the first time, it was mine. Following the right people in life makes a difference. We can choose to follow that which is righteous and prosper, and that's exactly what I did by following the words of James and Antonio.

CHAPTER 7

Finding Hope in Unexpected Places

Higb school did not feel like a fresh start. I walked into it carrying everything I had survived before. Reading was easier than it used to be because of James and Antonio, but it still did not come naturally. Every assignment required extra effort. Every test felt like a challenge waiting to expose me. I did not walk the halls feeling smart. I walked them praying nobody noticed where I still struggled.

But high school introduced me to something different: It introduced me to being seen. I had played football before: Little League, youth teams, neighborhood leagues; but stepping onto a high school football field was different. The space was bigger. The expectations were higher, and the lights made everything visible.

When I stepped onto that field, the rules were clear. Do your job. I remember the first practice clearly. The smell of grass. Cleats digging into dirt. Coaches shouting instructions from every direction. Teammates yelling encouragement. It was loud and chaotic, but it was a kind of chaos I understood.

Then came the moment that surprised me. I made a tackle. Nothing flashy. Just effort and instinct coming together. Coach Valliere blew the whistle and stared straight at me.

"Brown," he said, "where have you been hiding? We can use that."

It was the junior varsity team, but that did not matter to me. For the first time in a long time, an adult was not focusing on what I could not do. He was acknowledging what I brought.

I was no longer invisible. The locker room had its own atmosphere. The smell of sweat and worn pads. Cold metal lockers. Disinfectant barely covering the work of the day. To some people, it was just a room. To me, it was a proving ground. It was a place where excuses did not last long.

One afternoon after practice, I sat on the bench with my head down. I had missed assignments. I had blown a drill. Everything felt heavy. Around me, teammates laughed, joked, slapped helmets, and moved on. I stayed frozen in my disappointment.

That is when John McGee, better known as Toopoo, stepped in. He looked at me and said, "Man, stop moping. Get your ass in line. So what? Let's go."

No sympathy. No soft words. Just accountability.

We did not have a car back then, so we walked home after practice. That day, I lingered in the locker room longer than I should have, still stuck in my own head. Toopoo waited anyway. That was who he was.

By the end of the JV season, we both moved up to varsity. Toopoo adjusted immediately. I did not. The speed was faster. The hits were harder. The bodies were bigger. He became one of the hardest running backs in Broward County football, relentless and fearless. He ran like every carry mattered.

Years later, when I stood and eulogized him, I understood something I could not see then. He had already preached to me long before I ever stood behind a pulpit. He preached through toughness, loyalty, and truth spoken without apology.

My senior year brought a night I will never forget. We were playing Hollywood Hills High School. The bleachers were packed. The band shook the stands. The lights burned so bright, they erased everything beyond the field.

We were down by three. They were on our one-yard line. I bent over with my hands on my knees and tried to slow my breathing. Across from me stood Stevie Bryant, one of the best running backs in the county. He was calm and confident like the moment belonged to him.

3rd and 1.

The snap came. The ball was pitched. He came straight toward my side. I stepped forward, squared my shoulders, and reached out.

For a split second, I had him. Then I did not. He slipped past my grasp, turned the corner, and crossed the goal line. The stadium erupted. Their sideline exploded. I stood there frozen, staring at the end zone.

Touchdown.

By the final whistle, the scoreboard read ten to zero.

The walk back to the locker room felt longer than the game itself. No one talked. Cleats scraped against concrete. Shoulder pads hit the floor harder than usual. I sat at my locker and stared at the nameplate above it.

That missed tackle stayed with me.

For a long time, I believed that moment defined me. Like failure had stamped my identity. It took years to understand that it exposed something else instead. It exposed what I believed about myself.

High school football did not erase my struggles. It did something more important. It showed me what it felt like to be seen. It taught me accountability without cruelty. It showed me that failure could happen under bright lights and still not have the final word.

That field gave me confidence. That locker room shaped my character, and that missed tackle taught me humility. Hope did not arrive all at once. It began quietly. It took root in effort, correction, and moments that did not go my way. I did not know it then, but hope was already working in unexpected places.

CHAPTER 8

Becoming the Man I Didn't Know I Could Be

The bar felt heavier than usual that day.

I lay back on the bench, eyes locked on the steel above me, hands wrapped tight around the knurling. The room was loud. Plates clanked. Someone laughed across the room. A coach yelled at another group, but all of it faded as I pulled the weight off the rack.

Two hundred and fifty pounds.

I lowered the bar to my chest and felt it settle there, pressing the air out of my lungs. My arms shook as I pushed. Halfway up, doubt crept in. My elbows wavered. For a split second, I thought about racking it and calling it a day.

Then I heard it.

"Let's go, E!"

"Push it!"

I drove my feet into the floor and pressed again. My arms burned. My chest tightened. Slowly, the bar moved. Inch by inch, it rose until my elbows locked out.

The room erupted.

"Man, you're getting strong now!"

"Yeah, E!"

I racked the weight and sat up, heart pounding, sweat dripping down my face. It wasn't just the lift. It was what it proved. For the first time, I felt strong in a way that had nothing to do with football, grades, or anyone else's opinion.

High school didn't just change my schedule. It changed how I carried myself. Somewhere between classes, practices, and afternoons that felt louder than they needed to be, I stopped moving through the day like I was hoping not to be noticed. I didn't have everything figured out, but I wasn't shrinking anymore.

The weight room became my anchor.

It had its own rhythm. Plates clanking. Benches squeaking. Coaches barking encouragement that sounded more like commands than praise.

"Come on. Push it."

I loved it.

The rules made sense there. If you put in the work, the work paid you back. No guessing. No pretending. No hiding behind excuses. Just effort and response. That honesty mattered to me.

I didn't realize that the same concept applied to academics: if you put in the work, it will pay off in the long run. As a beginner in the weight room, I started out with very little to no muscle. Each rep felt like more than muscle being built. It felt like something was being stripped away. Doubt.

Hesitation. The quiet belief that I wasn't enough. The more consistent I became, the steadier I felt everywhere else.

I still struggled academically. That didn't disappear. But I stopped running from the effort. James and Antonio were still around, still sharp, still moving forward. They didn't slow down for me or explain things twice. They expected me to keep up. That expectation pulled more out of me than sympathy ever could.

I was growing physically in the weight room. I was growing mentally by refusing to quit. Confidence started to settle in, not loudly, not all at once, but in the way I stood straighter and spoke without rehearsing everything in my head first.

By my junior year, I was one of the stronger defensive backs on the team. More importantly, I had learned something the weight room teaches quietly, day after day. Repetition builds more than strength. It builds trust in yourself. It builds patience. It builds the ability to stay present when things get uncomfortable.

High school also introduced me to something lifting and football couldn't prepare me for.

Girls.

There was one girl whose smile changed the hallway every time I saw her. One morning, I noticed her struggling to carry two heavy textbooks. I didn't plan what I was going to say. I just said it.

"You need help with those?"

She smiled and said yes. I carried her books even though I wasn't headed that way. We talked the whole walk. She laughed at my jokes, most of which I probably borrowed from James. Still, the words felt like mine when I said them.

Nothing came of it. No relationship. No big moment, but it mattered. It was the first time I realized I didn't need borrowed confidence to speak. Sometimes, showing up was enough.

Even with all that growth, reading never completely left me alone. There were nights I stared at textbooks longer than I should have. The difference was that I wasn't stuck anymore. I was moving. Slowly. Steadily.

I started understanding more than I used to. Comprehension came in pieces, but it came. For the first time, graduation felt possible.

James crossed the stage in 1984. Antonio followed in 1985. That same year, I walked right behind him. It wasn't the path I imagined for myself, but it was the path I finished.

That diploma opened doors I didn't expect. A football scholarship took me to Fergus Falls, Minnesota. The cold shocked me the moment I stepped outside. My breath looked different up there. Football didn't.

After a year, I transferred to Bethune-Cookman College in Daytona Beach. I didn't play football there, but I learned how to stand on my own in a world bigger than the one I came from.

When life brought me back home, I noticed something quietly. I wasn't the same kid who walked into high school unsure of his place. I had learned how to work. How to stay. How to grow without needing permission.

I didn't have everything figured out, but I was no longer asking who I was allowed to be. I was becoming someone solid enough to find out.

CHAPTER 9

The Village That Raised Me

Growing up in Hollywood, Florida, in a neighborhood called Liberia, you learned early that survival was communal.

Liberia was one of Hollywood's oldest Black neighborhoods, born during segregation, when Black families were not allowed to live anywhere else. What started as restriction became something else over time. Families built homes, churches, schools, and relationships that held each other together. The name Liberia carried meaning. It spoke of freedom, pride, and the belief that even when options were limited, dignity was not.

Everything important to my childhood sat inside that community. Bethune Elementary. Attucks Middle School. The Teen Center. You didn't need a ride to find your way. You just needed to show up.

There was one place that shaped us more than any street corner or playground ever could.

The Teen Center.

Looking back now, that building was proof that the saying is true. It really does take a village to raise a child. For us, the Teen Center *was* the village.

As kids, it was our safe place. If we weren't at home or in school, we were there. Running across fields. Shooting basketballs until our arms were tired. Throwing footballs. Playing baseball. Sitting at long tables doing arts and crafts. Going on field trips. Being kids without having to look over our shoulders.

It gave childhood room to breathe.

The Teen Center kept us busy, but it also kept us seen. There were dances, cultural events, DJs playing music outside, and a steady stream of activities that pulled us in instead of pushing us away. I ran with my boys James and Antonio. We called James "Buddy" and Antonio "Yo," but it wasn't just us. It was a whole crew. Boys who became brothers through competition, laughter, and shared summers that felt endless.

What made the Teen Center different was not the building. It was the adults.

Miss Rose was the first center coordinator any of us really knew. She had a way of making the room feel safe just by being in it. I can still see myself sitting at those tables, fitting puzzle pieces together while she watched over us. She was a mother figure to all of us. She didn't just manage the space. She held it together.

In a community that carried heavy burdens, Miss Rose was soft enough to rest on and strong enough to support us. Everyone knew her. Everyone respected her. She made sure we felt protected.

When Miss Rose left, Percell Gregory stepped in.

Percell was steady. No-nonsense. The kind of man who didn't waste words. He coached our Little League team. He pushed us hard. He believed discipline mattered. Later, he gave me my very first recreation job. At the time, I didn't fully understand what that meant. Looking back, I see it clearly. He trusted me with responsibility before I fully trusted myself.

Percell was the kind of adult who showed love through consistency. Through showing up. Through expecting something from you.

Then there was Mr. Alvin Lightfoot.

Mr. Lightfoot didn't just teach games. He taught perspective. One afternoon, I explained to him that I was given the responsibility to head up a career day at an elementary school. Mr. Lightfoot gave me games to play that he created, but one of the most important games he taught me was life itself.

"If I give you a fish, you'll eat for a day," he said.

"But if I teach you how to fish…"

"I'll eat for a lifetime," I finished.

"That's right," he said. "Now get back on the court and keep learning. Losing ain't failure. It's education."

Mr. Lightfoot had a way of educating us even when we thought he was just speaking words. He didn't preach. He prepared. And though he's gone now, his words still surface when I need grounding.

In the background was Mr. Irvin Anderson. Quiet. Observant. Always working. One day I watched him mopping the floor. He noticed me watching and said, "Son, most people walk past problems. Leaders fix them." Then he handed me the broom.

No speech. No lesson plan. Just example.

That's how the Teen Center worked. You were taught by presence. By expectation. By being trusted enough to participate.

Those men and women didn't fix my reading struggles. They didn't erase my challenges. What they did was give me something just as important. Stability. Structure. Accountability. A place where I was seen for more than what I struggled with.

They shaped me before I knew I was being shaped.

I wasn't raised by one mentor. I was raised by a village. A village that believed in showing up. A village that stayed. A village that made room for kids like me to grow at our own pace without being written off.

Long before I understood purpose or calling, the Teen Center was teaching me how to stand, how to listen, and how to contribute. It didn't just keep me safe. It kept me connected.

Because of that village, I carried more than survival with me. I carried foundation.

CHAPTER 10

Crossing the Stage, Stepping Into the Unknown

Senior year was the year I had waited for my whole life, and the year I feared the most.

By 1985, I had survived thirteen long years of school. From Bethune Elementary, to Attucks Middle, to the halls of South Broward High School, I carried more than notebooks and gym bags. I carried the quiet weight of reading below level. Every test, every assignment, every report card reminded me that I was running a race with weights on my ankles. Graduation was approaching, and I still didn't know if I had enough to cross the finish line.

When grades came out that spring, they weren't mailed home or emailed. They were posted on a wall. Your future, public and unavoidable.

I remember slowing my steps as I walked toward it. My heart was pounding so hard it felt like it echoed in the hallway. Part of me wanted to turn around, pretend I didn't care, pretend I didn't need that moment. But something pushed me forward.

Then I saw it.

My name.

On the wall.

Listed with the graduates.

I froze. Then I smiled. Then I said thank you out loud right there in the hallway, not caring who heard me. I didn't fully understand what that moment meant yet. I only knew I had crossed a line I once believed I never would.

I had the ability to play at a major university, but my SAT scores and core grades said otherwise. That reality redirected my path to junior college. At the time, it felt like being overlooked. Like being underestimated. I didn't have language for it then. I just knew the door I wanted wasn't opening.

One afternoon, while sitting in science class, the head football coach, who also happened to be the teacher, called me over. He asked me to take a recruiter down to the film room and show him Antonio's highlights.

While the tape played, the coach paused the screen. He kept staring at one jersey number.

Mine.

He looked at me and said, "I might not be able to get Antonio, but I'd like to take a look at this guy."

For a moment, the room felt different. Possibility hung in the air. Someone was watching me. Someone important.

Then reality followed. I didn't have the grades. And truthfully, I wasn't ready for that level, mentally or academically.

The opportunity was real, but so were my limitations. I didn't know how to process that yet. I only knew it hurt.

Graduation didn't feel like an ending. It felt like standing at the edge of something unfamiliar.

Leaving South Florida for Fergus Falls, Minnesota was the biggest jump of my life. I wasn't going there for academics. I was going to play football. That was the one place where things still made sense when reading didn't.

I arrived before the snow and thought I could handle it. Then winter came.

The cold in Minnesota wasn't the kind you feel. It was the kind that finds you. The kind that makes you question whether you belong. Before long, even football couldn't distract me from the shock of it all. Confidence slipped. Motivation faded. Loneliness crept in quietly and stayed.

Minnesota was nothing like South Florida. The weather, the culture, the pace of life. Everything felt foreign. My roommate was a white kid from a small rural town who had never seen a Black person in real life before. Never. And there we were, sharing a room, trying to make sense of each other.

At first, it was awkward. Sometimes uncomfortable. But time has a way of forcing conversation. Curiosity replaced silence. Familiarity replaced distance.

That year stretched me. Snowstorms. Quiet nights. Cultural shock. I didn't have words for what was happening to me yet. I only knew I was changing.

Minnesota wasn't just about football. It was about learning how to survive away from everything I knew.

When I look back on that season, I see a young man carrying far more than books. I was carrying fear, insecurity, and the frustration of still not reading on level. Yet somehow, even with all that weight, I kept moving forward.

Graduation wasn't just a ceremony. It was proof I could finish something.

Minnesota wasn't just a destination. It was unfamiliar ground that demanded growth.

Football was the reason I left home. What I gained there would take longer to understand.

Even then, I didn't know how to read the story of my life. I was just living it.

It took time, but I understand that nothing in that season was wasted. The doors that opened, the ones that closed, and the distance between them were all shaping something I didn't yet have language for.

I couldn't read the story then, but the story was still being written.

CHAPTER 11

When the Road Turns Back Home

In 1986, I made a decision that felt like a fresh start. I left Fergus Falls, Minnesota, and headed to Bethune-Cookman College in Daytona Beach, Florida. After surviving the cold, the culture shock, and the distance from home, I was ready for something familiar. Something warm. Something Black. Something that felt like me.

But one thing came with me that I couldn't shake.

I still wasn't reading on level.

No matter what school I stepped into, that struggle followed me like a shadow. And even though my dream had always been to play football, that dream had quietly faded. I had no offers. No coaches calling. No recruiters waiting. And if I'm honest, I didn't want to keep playing anymore. My heart just wasn't in it.

I told myself I was at Bethune for a degree, but my actions told a different story. I rarely went to class, but I never missed a party. I showed up to every step show, every football game, every basketball game. With the ratio being nine women to every one man on campus, my priorities were not academic.

Bethune-Cookman gave me culture, connection, and a sense of belonging. It also gave me distraction. I learned how to party. I learned how to drink. I learned how to chase excitement instead of discipline. I learned lessons the hard way.

In the middle of all that, I met Miss Baker.

She was one of the reading instructors on campus, and from the beginning, she saw something in me that I didn't see in myself. Every single day, she would come to my dorm, walk me back to her office, sit me down, and place a list of words in front of me. She refused to let me quit. She refused to let me hide.

She helped me read. She pushed me to improve. She held me accountable. She even took me with her to mentor middle school students, teaching me responsibility before I understood what responsibility really meant. Miss Baker didn't just teach me words. She taught me discipline. She taught me consistency. She taught me what it felt like to have someone believe in me when I didn't believe in myself.

Although I didn't graduate from Bethune-Cookman, the year-and-a-half I spent there changed me. My reading improved because she stayed committed to me even when I wasn't committed to myself. That alone is why I will always recommend an HBCU to every African-American young person. The culture, the people, and the environment gave me something no other school could have.

Miss Baker kept pushing me to become a better student. One day, she suggested I enroll in ROTC. What I didn't realize at the time was that ROTC at Bethune-Cookman wasn't just a class, it was run by the U.S. Army.

Every Tuesday and Thursday morning, physical training started between 4:30 and 5:00 a.m. Like clockwork, ROTC cadets would pound on my dorm-room door. That routine didn't sit well with my roommate, Christopher T. Hart, better known as Dirty Hart. One morning, the knocking woke him before it woke me. Chris jumped out of bed in a full rage. He was about 6'6" and pushing close to 300 pounds. After a stern, unforgettable lecture, those ROTC guys never knocked again. Then he turned to me and said, "Get your ass up. You hear them knocking."

One morning during PT, we were told we'd be running to the Daytona 500 racetrack. When we finally arrived, they told us we'd need to run one or two laps around the track. If you know anything about that racetrack, you know it's no short run. Let's just say I eventually made my way home.

Later, I asked Miss Baker why she pushed me into ROTC in the first place. Her answer was simple. She wanted to boost my GPA. And while it was the hardest "C" I ever earned, it was also one of the most valuable grades of my life. ROTC gave me structure, accountability, and perseverance, lessons that stayed with me long after the early mornings were over.

One evening on my way to dinner, I stopped near the cafeteria where a white woman stood handing out credit card applications. She asked if I was a student and if I had a home address. When I said yes, she told me it was my lucky day.

A week later, my first Discover card arrived in the mail. I tried to use it at the ABC liquor store, but the card didn't work. The cashier shook her head and said, "Boy, you can't use this card." When I asked why, she said, "Because you never activated it."

I ran back to the dorm, not realizing there was a phone booth right outside the store. I called the 1-800 number on the back of the card, followed the steps, and activated it. Then I went back and used it. That moment stuck with me.

Eventually, the partying, the trouble, and a few fights caught up with me. It became clear my time at Bethune-Cookman had come to an end. I went back home and slept on my sister's couch, sometimes in the same room as my nieces, for the next few years.

It wasn't glamorous. It wasn't comfortable. But it was necessary.

That season wasn't about success. It was about survival. It wasn't about rising. It was about being rebuilt.

CHAPTER 12

The Beginning of Us

I remember the first time I heard someone say, "Opposites attract." It sounded clever, maybe even poetic, but it didn't mean anything to me at the time. Not until I met Shari Pinkney.

Shari and I were nothing alike. I loved drinking, partying, laughing loud, staying out late, and drifting through life without much direction. Shari loved reading, writing, going to church, staying grounded, and thinking deeply. Where I was wild, she was consistent. Where I was reckless, she was steady. Where I was chaos, she was calm.

At the time, I didn't have language for why she felt so different to me. I only knew she did.

Shari and I technically went to the same elementary school, though I have no memory of her from those days. She insists she remembers me, mostly because I was the "bad student." I don't argue with that. She's probably right.

What she didn't know then, and what I didn't yet know how to explain, was that much of my behavior came from my inability to read. I didn't know how to ask for help, and I didn't know how to hide my struggle quietly. So I acted out. Being labeled "bad" became a distraction, a way to pull attention away from what I couldn't do and toward what I could control. Every joke, every disruption, every trip to the principal's office was really covering up fear and shame.

I wasn't a bad kid. I was a kid without a voice. And until I found the courage and tools to express what I was carrying, trouble spoke for me.

Years later, life had moved on, and so had I. Every week, my fraternity hosted a car wash fundraiser. We'd be out there scrubbing rims, spraying suds, cracking jokes, and raising a little money. One day, a gray Toyota Tercel pulled up, and Shari stepped out.

After that first wash, it became a running joke.

"Hey, E, here's that gray Toyota Tercel!"

"Ain't nobody touching that car but E!"

To them, it was harmless flirting. To me, it felt like something shifting. From where I stood, that gray Toyota wasn't just pulling into a car wash. It was pulling into my life.

Now, if you ask Shari, or my sister—my cousin who my mama raised as my sister—Deborah McGee, you'll hear a different version of that story. Their version includes more details and a lot more honesty than I'm ready to put in print. But this is my chapter, and this is how I remember it.

Before I go any further, I have to say this about Deborah.

When I came home from college with no job, no degree, and no direction, Deborah opened her home to me. I didn't pay rent. I didn't contribute groceries. I just lived there. Free.

She took care of me during a season when I had very little to offer. That kind of love leaves a mark. I owe her more than I can ever repay, and I will love her for the rest of my life.

Back to Shari.

The truth is, when I met her, I was already in a relationship with someone else. Then, just weeks later, Pam passed away. Sudden. Shocking. Heavy. Loss settled in, and in the middle of that grief, something in me still recognized peace when I saw it.

I remember telling my sister, "Shari is going to be my wife."

It sounded bold. Maybe even reckless. But there was something about her presence that calmed parts of me I didn't know how to quiet. Being around her made me want to be better, even when I didn't yet know how.

One Saturday, I asked my father to go with me to the jewelry store. I needed him to sign for the ring. My credit wasn't worth much of anything. Without hesitation, he signed. He didn't just co-sign a purchase. He gave his blessing.

Ring in hand, I went to see James, my best friend. We celebrated the moment the only way we knew how, drinking, then plotting the proposal. We called Shari over. She arrived. I rehearsed everything I wanted to say.

Before I could say a word, she saw the ring.

That was the proposal.

Despite the awkwardness, she said yes.

Her mother wasn't thrilled. The church wasn't thrilled either. When our engagement was announced, people grumbled out loud. To them, Shari was light. I was a drunk. A troublemaker. A question mark.

But love has a way of moving forward anyway.

We dated another year, then planned our wedding. Shari cared deeply about every detail. Colors. Seating. Timing. Flow. I just wanted to stand at the altar, say "I do," and celebrate.

We planned for 300 people. More than 500 showed up.

A bus from Charleston pulled up full of family who hadn't received invitations. People stood through the ceremony. Food ran out. The plan collapsed.

But the love didn't.

That day taught me something I didn't learn from books or sermons. Not everything meaningful fits inside a plan. Love makes room. Hospitality stretches. Community overflows.

After marriage came fatherhood. Shari already had a daughter, Precious. Becoming her stepfather changed me in ways I didn't expect. Years later, when I watched her graduate high school and earn her AA degree through dual enrollment, I cried. I saw discipline. Focus. Possibility. She didn't just graduate. She awakened something in me.

Months later, I earned my own AA degree.

Then came Erica.

The night she was born, everything shifted. Holding her in my arms, I felt responsibility settle in a way nothing else ever had. I still struggled with reading. But now I had a family depending on me. So I made a choice. Quietly. Intentionally. I began teaching myself. Reading alone. Studying in silence. Taking online classes. One word at a time.

Then one day, the phone rang.

Shari worked in the church's financial ministry, and pastors usually called asking for her. This time, it was a new pastor, Pastor Eddie Lake. When I heard his voice, I said "Shari your pastor is on the phone".

"I did not call to speak to her. I called to speak to the man of the house," he said.

No one had ever called me that before. That moment stayed with me. It wasn't loud. It wasn't dramatic. But it marked something. I wasn't just living in a house anymore. I was learning how to lead a home.

Looking back now, I see a pattern I didn't recognize then. Love didn't just give me companionship. It gave me responsibility. Fatherhood didn't just give me children. It gave me purpose. And being called the man of the house didn't just name a role. It called something forward in me that had been quiet for a long time.

Meeting Shari didn't just begin a relationship. It began the long work of becoming.

CHAPTER 13

Meeting Jesus

It was February 6, 2005. Super Bowl Sunday. The New England Patriots were playing the Philadelphia Eagles in Super Bowl XXXIX, and like most people that night, I was focused on the game, the drinks, and the atmosphere. I had been invited to a Super Bowl party at Ed Darling's house, one of the biggest homes in the neighborhood. Ed was a successful home developer, a man who had built well and lived well, and I was excited to be there. Looking back now, I still speak his name with gratitude and love, praying continued blessing over his family.

During the third quarter of the game, something shifted inside me. I poured myself another drink and wandered into Ed's living room, taking in the space, the craftsmanship, the feeling of success that filled the room. Ed walked in behind me and said, in his deep, confident voice,

"Hey brother, you like this?"

I smiled and answered honestly.

"You better believe I like it."

But then a question rose up in me, unfiltered and raw, and I asked it quietly in my spirit.

"God, why can't I have a house like this?"

As I walked toward the kitchen to fix another drink, I heard a still, unmistakable voice say,

"You're done."

I had been in church before, but I did not truly know Jesus. This was not religion speaking, and it was not my conscience bargaining with me. The message was clear and heavy. If I wanted a life like the one I admired, it would cost me the life I was living. Not physical death, but the end of my old patterns, my old habits, and my old identity.

I did not stay until the end of the game. Before the final whistle ever blew, I left the party and went home, crying. Super Bowl Sunday was usually a long night for me, one that stretched until two or three in the morning. That night, I walked through my front door early, overwhelmed by something I could not yet explain. It was the first time silence had spoken louder than noise in my life.

When I walked in, my wife knew something was wrong. She looked at me with confusion because she knew I never came home that early. She didn't know what had happened at the party, but she could see that something had changed. That night, God did not simply interrupt my routine. He confronted me, invited me, and began dismantling the life I thought I needed.

That night marked the beginning of my relationship with Jesus, but it also marked the beginning of finding my voice. Until then, my voice had been shaped by noise, approval, and performance. I spoke loudly in rooms but quietly in my soul, using sound to cover the absence of direction. When God spoke to me, He didn't raise His volume; He sharpened my awareness. For the first time, I was responding instead of reacting.

I didn't preach that night. I didn't pray aloud. I didn't even fully understand what had happened. All I did was go home early and sit with the weight of that moment. But something had shifted, and my old voice was losing its power. A new one was beginning to form, not through speaking, but through listening.

Although I met Jesus that night, my struggle with drinking did not end immediately. I stopped for a season, but in my mind, it was only a pause. I fully expected to return to it later, believing I was still in control. What I didn't realize was that while I was making plans, my steps were already being redirected.

As the weeks passed, my wife began questioning the amount of money I was spending on alcohol. Instead of confronting the habit itself, I looked for a workaround. I decided to get a part-time job, not to change my life, but to fund the very thing that was slowly draining it. My logic was simple: if I earned extra money, no one could question how I spent it.

The job I found was at a group home for troubled teenage boys. I worked weekends, organizing activities and supervising the young men. One rule was non-negotiable. Every Sunday morning, everyone went to church. No exceptions. So every week, I loaded up a van full of teenage boys and drove them to Mt. Bethel Baptist Church, where Bishop Glover was the pastor.

More times than I care to admit, I walked into that church hung over from the night before. My body was tired, my head was foggy, but something kept pulling me back. Week after week, Bishop Glover preached with clarity and conviction that reached places alcohol never could. After a few months, I noticed something changing. I stayed out less on Saturday nights, not because I was trying to change, but because I didn't want to miss the message on Sunday morning.

By the fifth month, I stopped going out altogether. What I thought was a job meant to sustain my addiction became a disruption to it. A group of troubled boys, a mandatory church rule, and a faithful pastor became the framework that slowly redirected my life. I didn't plan it that way, but the shift was undeniable.

Around that same time, I began attending church every Sunday with my wife at Greater Mount Pleasant AME Church in Hollywood, Florida. For years she had pleaded with me to attend faithfully, and my presence had always been inconsistent. Now, church was no longer a place I visited occasionally. It became a place where I belonged.

My second encounter with the Holy Spirit happened publicly. There was a special program at Greater Mount Pleasant AME Church, and I asked my supervisor if I could bring the boys from the group home with me that Sunday. A visiting evangelist preached and invited anyone who felt called to come forward. I was preparing to leave when the evangelist said,

"I'm not stopping until the one God is calling comes forward."

Then he added words that cut straight through me. I began sweating, frozen in my seat, knowing exactly who he was talking to. Conviction overtook me, and I walked to the altar. He prophesied over me, calling out my past and pointing toward a future I had never imagined for myself.

After that moment, growth followed. My reading improved. My academic confidence increased. I began reading the Bible daily, and for the first time, the words made sense to me. That spiritual growth led me back to school, where I enrolled at American InterContinental University and completed my associate degree in business administration in eight months.

Not long after, Pastor Lake invited me to join the church's evangelism team. We went into the very neighborhoods where I had once been known for drinking and partying. Some of the men laughed when they saw me and said,

"Stop playing with God. You know you not serious."

But I kept showing up. Evangelism became the first place my new voice felt natural. It wasn't polished, but it was honest.

As time went on, the calling expanded. Pastor Lake poured into me, traveling with me to places like Houston and Birmingham, teaching me how to share the gospel. I went on my first missionary trip to Jamaica, where I witnessed more than one hundred people give their lives to Christ. I ministered in prisons and preached in churches, growing more confident with every step.

Eventually, I approached leadership about becoming an evangelist in the AME Church. Over two years, I was denied three times. Some reasons were clear, others were not. I didn't understand it then, but I knew I was being told no. What I did understand was that the door hadn't opened yet.

CHAPTER 14

Faithful in the City: Learning to Lead Where I Was Planted

Long before titles, pulpits, or invitations to preach, my leadership was being shaped quietly in the city of Hollywood, Florida. I did not begin there with authority or recognition. I began as a recreational aide in 1997, learning the basics of service, accountability, and consistency. Over time, that role expanded into greater responsibility, eventually leading me to serve as a parks and recreation manager. The work was demanding, detailed, and often unseen, but it taught me how to lead without applause.

Balancing full-time work while pursuing my bachelor's degree was one of the most challenging seasons of my life. My responsibilities with the City of Hollywood required constant attention, from park inspections and staff supervision to meetings with boards and city commissioners. Every day demanded preparation, professionalism, and patience. There were no shortcuts. The work required diligence, and it revealed quickly whether I was dependable or merely ambitious.

My journey with the City of Hollywood reminded me often of *The Tortoise and the Hare*. I did not move quickly, but I moved faithfully. Over the course of thirty-one years, I watched positions change, leadership shift, and opportunities rise and fall. Though my desire to become parks director never materialized there, I remain deeply grateful for the city that shaped my work ethic and strengthened my resolve. Each role prepared me for responsibility beyond job descriptions.

In 2018, when the parks director retired, I considered pursuing the interim assistant director position. I was cautioned to be careful about what I asked for when I asked to be considered for the assistant parks director position.

After prayer and reflection, I chose to release the opportunity and trust the process unfolding in my life. Not long after, I applied for the Parks Director position with the City of Dania Beach. Fear nearly caused me to withdraw my application, uncertain about leaving a place I had served for decades. Yet when the offer came, clarity followed. I accepted, trusting the next step.

My time in Dania Beach affirmed everything Hollywood had taught me. In five years, our team planned and initiated projects that brought meaningful impact to the community, including the development of a facility valued at over $20 million in my parents' neighborhood. These accomplishments were not individual victories. They were the result of collaboration, vision, and steady leadership.

When Ana Garcia became city manager, many anticipated difficulty due to her reputation. Manager Garcia was one of the most affectionate people I've ever met. Very firm but fair, not only did we develop a great working relationship, but we also developed a great friendship in Christ. I am grateful that she placed her trust in me. Our early interactions were direct and challenging. Yet through honest conversation and accountability, a strong professional respect developed. I remained the only director who stayed through leadership transitions, not because of comfort, but because of commitment. That season reinforced a truth I had learned long ago: leadership is sustained by trust, not titles.

I share this chapter not to recount a career, but to testify to the importance of stewardship. The city became my classroom long before the church became my platform. Hollywood and Dania Beach taught me how to lead people, manage responsibility, and remain faithful where I was planted. Long before my voice was heard publicly, it was tested daily through service.

This chapter of my life confirmed something essential. Leadership is not proven by where you speak, but by how you serve. And the voice God was forming in me was strengthened as much in city hall as it ever would be in a sanctuary.

CHAPTER 15

The Long Road to Finding My Voice

In 2011, I received a phone call that changed the trajectory of my calling. Pastor Moise, who served as the Dean of the Board of Examiners, informed me that Bishop Richardson had adjusted the standards. Even though I did not yet hold a bachelor's degree, I was being granted permission to appear before the Board during my very first year on trial. I understood immediately that this opportunity did not come from human favor. It was an opening I had not earned, but one I was being trusted to steward.

When I stood before the Board of Examiners for the first time, I did so with humility and awareness. I knew I was walking into a sacred space that carried expectation, accountability, and scrutiny. This was not a shortcut, and it was not a reward. It was a test of obedience. I accepted the opportunity, knowing that saying yes meant committing myself fully to the process ahead, no matter how demanding it became.

That first year made one thing very clear. If I wanted to continue forward, higher education was not optional. Seminary would come later, but first things first, I needed a bachelor's degree. The requirement was not presented as punishment or delay. It was presented as preparation, and I chose to receive it that way.

I enrolled at Warner University and committed myself to earning a degree in Transformational Ministry. Balancing work, study, and ministry was not easy, but I had learned by then that progress did not come through speed. It came through consistency. I showed up, did the work, and kept moving forward even when the process felt slow.

In the spring of 2016, my wife and I drove to Lake Wales, Florida, for my graduation. Somewhere along that drive, the weight of the moment settled in. Most people earn a bachelor's degree within four or five years after high school. It had taken me thirty-one. Yet instead of feeling behind, I felt anchored. I had not quit. I had endured.

As we continued down the road, a familiar truth came back to me: the race is not given to the swift, nor the battle to the strong, but to the one who endures to the end. I thought about how many times my journey had been delayed, redirected, or misunderstood. And yet, here I was, still standing, still moving, still answering the call placed on my life.

I have often said that my favorite "book" outside of the Bible is *The Tortoise and the Hare*. We all know how that race ends. Not with speed, but with persistence. That realization stayed with me as I crossed the stage. My voice, which had once felt dormant and uncertain, was no longer waiting to be discovered. It was alive, formed through obedience, endurance, and time.

Earning my bachelor's degree did not signal the end of the process. It signaled the next instruction. Once I completed my studies at Warner University, the Board of Examiners made it clear that the next step was seminary. There was no debate and no delay. If I wanted to continue walking forward in this calling, I would need to submit myself fully to deeper study and formation.

I enrolled at Asbury Theological Seminary in Orlando, Florida. I showed up willing, but I also showed up uncertain. I did the work, attended classes, and engaged the material, yet something inside me never quite settled. I could not explain it at the time. All I knew was that while I was learning, I did not feel rooted. The environment was good, but it did not feel like where I was meant to finish.

Eventually, I was introduced to an online seminary based in Raleigh, North Carolina, Shaw University. After prayer and reflection, I made the decision to transfer. This time, the fit felt different. The instruction, the culture, and the pace aligned with where I was in life. I committed myself to the work with clarity and intention, determined not just to enroll, but to complete what I had started.

In May of 2024, I earned my Master of Divinity degree. Another milestone. Another door opened. But more than anything, it marked a pattern that had taken decades to develop. I had learned how to finish. What once felt impossible now felt earned through persistence, discipline, and steady obedience.

While studying at Shaw University, I encountered people who carried faith, purpose, and vision. We formed connections that extended beyond the classroom, and together we began traveling. These journeys were not about tourism. They were about exposure, growth, and understanding that calling does not exist in isolation.

Our travels took us first to Greece. Walking those streets carried a different weight than anything I had experienced before. History was no longer something I read about or heard preached. It was under my feet. I stood near what is believed to be Paul's prison, aware of how much suffering had shaped the faith I now carried freely. I read Scripture aloud in Corinth, not as performance, but as participation in something far older than myself.

Watching my wife step into the waters where Paul baptized Lydia was another moment that settled deeply into me. There was no need for commentary or explanation. The moment spoke for itself. Faith was no longer abstract. It was embodied. It was geographic. It was real in a way that required reverence rather than interpretation.

London offered a different kind of testing. There, I was asked to share a devotion with a group of believers traveling together. Standing before them, I felt the familiar awareness of responsibility. This was not about being impressive. It was about being faithful. The words came without force or strain. I spoke plainly, clearly, and with purpose. I realized afterward that I was no longer borrowing language or confidence. I was speaking from lived understanding.

What struck me most in those moments was not where I was standing, but who I was becoming while standing there. I was not trying to prove anything. I was simply doing the work set in front of me. The voice that once struggled to form sentences was now steady enough to carry meaning across cultures and contexts.

These experiences did not elevate me. They clarified me. They showed me that the voice I had worked so hard to develop was not meant to stay hidden or theoretical. It was meant to be used, tested, and refined in real spaces with real people.

By this point, I understood something without needing to name it. My voice had not been lost in earlier years. It had been forming. and now, it was being trusted with responsibility beyond familiarity or comfort.

By the time these experiences began to converge, I no longer felt the need to announce what I was becoming. The work itself made that clear. Education had given me structure. Travel had given me perspective. Experience had given me confidence. But none of it mattered unless I could carry responsibility consistently, without applause, without shortcuts, and without losing myself in the process.

What stood out most during this season was not where I was invited to go, but how I was expected to show up. Whether in classrooms, churches, or unfamiliar spaces, the expectation was the same. Be prepared. Be present. Be accountable. I was no longer operating in moments. I was operating in rhythm.

The discipline I had learned through years of delay was now required daily.

I began to recognize that leadership does not arrive as a sudden promotion. It arrives quietly through trust. People trusted me with their time, their stories, their questions, and their faith. That trust carried weight. It demanded consistency, clarity, and humility. I was no longer speaking to be heard. I was speaking because responsibility required it.

This season also forced me to reconcile my past with my present. The years of struggle with reading, the long path through education, the delays and denials, none of those disappeared. Instead, they became reference points. They reminded me to stay patient, grounded, and aware of how easily confidence can turn into presumption if it is not anchored in discipline.

I realized then that the voice I had been working to develop was not meant for moments of inspiration alone. It was meant for sustained leadership. It needed to hold up under pressure, disagreement, fatigue, and expectation. That kind of voice is not formed quickly. It is earned through endurance.

Looking back, it became clear that this chapter of my life was not about arrival. It was about alignment. Everything I had walked through—education, testing, confirmation, exposure—had been shaping me for long-term responsibility rather than short-term recognition. The work itself had become the assignment.

This was the point where I understood something fully. Finding my voice was never about volume. It was about reliability. It was about being able to show up, speak clearly, and carry what I had been entrusted with, over time, without needing to prove that I belonged.

The process had done its work.

CHAPTER 16

My First Charge

I was ordained as an itinerant Deacon in September 2018, with every expectation that I would continue serving at Greater Mount Pleasant. I was still in the middle of the Board of Examiners process, still learning, still preparing, still very much in formation. Ministry felt demanding, but familiar. Nothing suggested that my life was about to shift in a way I could not manage or anticipate.

That changed in November 2018.

I was attending an evening program in Palm Beach County when I crossed paths with Presiding Elder Harvin. Our conversation was brief, almost casual. He asked how evangelism was going, and I told him honestly that it was going well and that I would gladly assist his district in evangelistic efforts if needed. He nodded, paused for a moment, and said, "That sounds great." Then he asked a question that would redirect my life.

"Would you go to Macedonia?"

At the time, I understood Macedonia to mean outreach, revival services, and temporary assignment. Evangelism was my comfort zone. I knew how to go in, preach, sow seed, and move on. What I did not realize was that this invitation was not about evangelism at all. It was about pastoring.

I learned that quickly.

Presiding Elder Harvin was not sending me to assist Macedonia AME Church. He was sending me to lead it. I did not yet have my Master of Divinity degree. I was not an elder in the AME Church. I was a full-time employee, a full-time student, and now being asked to take on what would become a full-time pastoral assignment. The weight of that realization settled immediately, and the pressure was undeniable.

I had never desired to be a pastor.

Evangelism allowed movement. Pastoring required staying. It required responsibility, consistency, and care beyond a single service or moment. Yet the more I prayed, the clearer it became that this assignment was not aligned with my preferences, but with my obedience. I had said, "Send me, and I will go," without understanding that going sometimes means remaining.

When I arrived at Macedonia, I did not arrive alone. My cousin, Pastor Troy, had served faithfully before me, and his leadership had already prepared the soil. He left behind structure, standards, and a congregation open to ministry. I stepped into an assignment that had been tended with integrity, and for that, I was grateful. I was not starting from nothing. I was building upon faithfulness.

My first Saturday at the church is still vivid. My wife and I met with a member who opened the building and walked us through the space. There was no formal gathering, no presentation, no ceremony. Yet the warmth we received eased much of my anxiety. Still, I understood early on that ministry is not sustained by welcome alone. It is sustained by endurance.

The first six months brought noticeable growth. New faces appeared, energy filled the room, and hope felt tangible. Over time, attendance plateaued. Sundays settled into ten or fifteen people, and frustration crept in. I prayed, evangelized monthly, and waited. What I learned in that season was simple but sobering: fruit does not move on our timetable.

That was when the idea of backyard services emerged.

Quarterly, we gathered behind the church in the vacant lot. I preached briefly, fifteen to twenty minutes at most. Food followed. Music filled the space. People laughed, danced, and stayed. Attendance at those services often surpassed our Sunday worship. It reminded me that the message does not change, but the methods can. People responded when ministry met them where they were.

My heart was also drawn to Florida Atlantic University. I visited the campus, built relationships with students, and invited them to serve and worship with us. Some attended. Others helped with outreach. We fed them, supported them, and sent them back to campus with what we could give. It affirmed what I already believed: investing in young people is not optional. It is essential.

Throughout all of this, Sis. Martin stood faithfully beside me. She ensured services flowed, worship continued, and needs were met. When musicians came and later departed, she adapted without complaint. Her service extended beyond the sanctuary into the community, visiting homes, delivering food, and helping people stay housed. She lived the gospel quietly and consistently.

When Sis. Martin passed away a few years later, I was already assigned to my second charge in Georgia and could not attend her service. Her absence was deeply felt. Her faithfulness remains a standard I carry with me.

My wife and I spent five years at Macedonia AME Church. When the time came to leave for Georgia, the final service became something sacred. There was a family in the congregation who had not spoken to one another for years. I personally invited each of them to attend. One woman, who had never attended church during my entire pastorate, agreed to come because it would be my last service.

She came.

That day, reconciliation unfolded. Tears were shed. Conversations long avoided finally happened. Relationships were restored. The service became less about departure and more about healing. It reminded me that ministry is not measured by numbers, but by transformation.

Macedonia was not simply my first charge. It was where obedience reshaped my understanding of leadership. I learned that authority grows through consistency, that a voice strengthens through responsibility, and that calling matures when we stay where we are sent. I did not arrive fully formed. I arrived willing.

And that was enough.

CHAPTER 17

Unspoken Struggles Find a Voice

This book is called *Unspoken Struggles* because for most of my life, that is exactly how I lived. I carried things I did not know how to explain. I struggled with reading, confidence, and direction, but I did not have the words to say what was really happening. So I stayed quiet, or I acted out, or I kept moving without slowing down long enough to face it.

For a long time, I thought my struggle meant I had no voice. I believed that if I could not speak clearly, read well, or move as fast as others, then my voice did not matter. What I learned over time is that silence does not mean absence. It means something is still forming.

My voice did not show up all at once. It grew slowly through work, discipline, and responsibility. It grew through education that took longer than planned. It grew through leadership I did not feel ready for. It grew through obedience when I did not fully understand what God was doing.

The struggles I kept unspoken were not wasted. They taught me patience. They taught me how to listen before speaking. They taught me how to stay steady when things were uncomfortable. Those same struggles are what gave my voice weight. I could speak honestly because I had lived honestly.

Finding your voice does not mean the struggle disappears. It means the struggle no longer controls you. It means you learn how to speak from experience instead of fear. My voice came from doing the work, not avoiding it.

If you are reading this and carrying things you have never said out loud, I want you to know this: your struggle is not the end of your story. It may be the beginning of your voice. You do not need to rush it. You do not need to hide it. You need to keep growing.

Unspoken Struggles is not just my story. It is proof that what you carry quietly can still lead you forward. A voice does not come from perfection. It comes from endurance.

My struggles were unspoken for a long time. They speak now and so will yours.

Those same unspoken struggles carried me farther than I ever imagined. They did not disqualify me from growth; they became the ground where growth took place. Through persistence and obedience, I earned an associate of arts degree, a bachelor's degree, and a master's degree, each one achieved at a pace that taught me humility, discipline, and faith. What once made me feel behind became the proof that delay is not denial.

Those struggles also opened doors of service and leadership. They allowed me to work in two different states as a parks and recreation director, serving communities with integrity and purpose. They led me into pastoral ministry, where I was entrusted to serve God's people as a senior pastor, first in Florida at Macedonia AME Church, and now at Saint Paul AME Church in Black Creek, Georgia. Every assignment stretched me, but every assignment also confirmed that a voice shaped by struggle carries authority.

This book is for anyone who has ever felt silenced by circumstance, learning challenges, fear, failure, or delay. If you feel like you do not have a voice, for whatever reason, this book is for you. Your struggle does not disqualify you from impact. It may be the very thing preparing you for it.

Unspoken Struggles is not just my story. It is evidence that what you carry quietly can still lead you boldly. A voice does not come from perfection. It comes from endurance. And endurance, when paired with faith, will always find its way to the surface.

www.ingramcontent.com/pod-product-compliance
Lightning Source LLC
Chambersburg PA
CBHW020330130626
46549CB00003B/1103